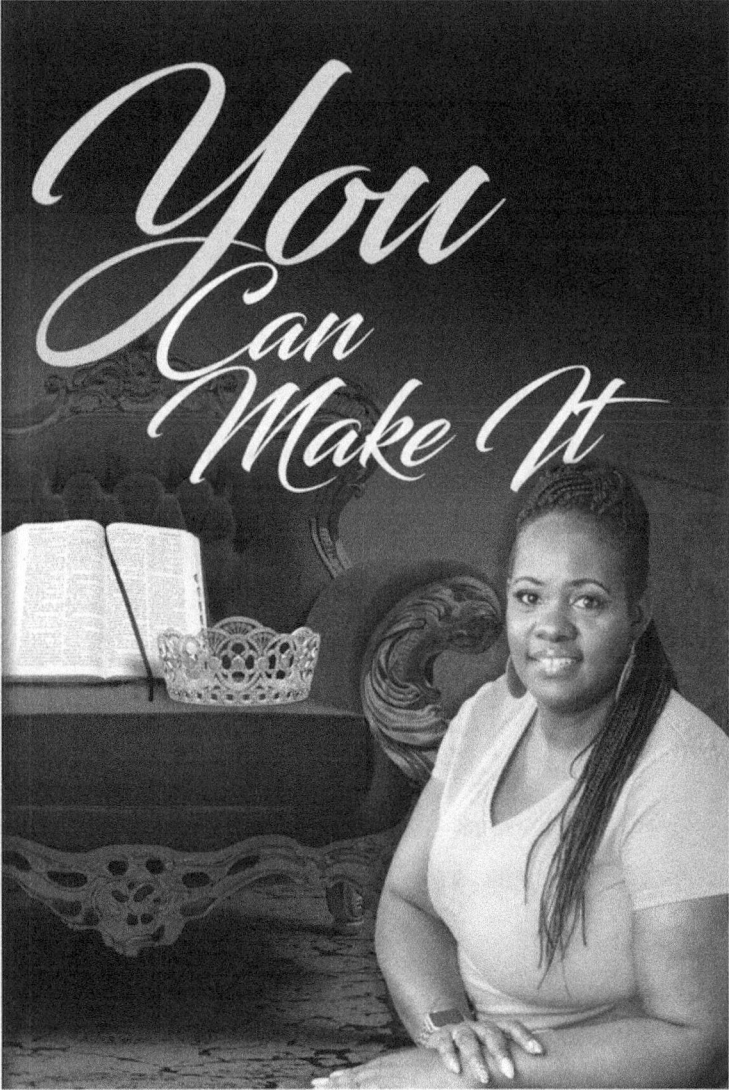

YOU CAN MAKE IT!

Vanessa Ray

Copyright © 2017 by Vanessa Ray

ISBN: 978-0692881804

Library of Congress Control Number: 2017906258

Cover Concept and Design by: Brian Harris & SD Horton Enterprises

Publishing, Editing, Formatting by: SD Horton Enterprises

SD
Horton
ENTERPRISES

www.sdhortonenterprises.com

Empowering the World through Inspiration

TABLE OF CONTENTS

ACKNOWLEDGMENTS

I would like to thank my publisher, Stacey Horton, for his guidance and leading me in the right direction.

Thanks to Intown Imagery for the photos.

Makeup by Tarayla Ray (my daughter).

Thanks to all of my grandkids whom I love dearly. They inspire me to leave a legacy for them.

I thank God for giving me the vision and creativity to tell my story. He gets all the glory! I was a wretch undone, lost, and broken into pieces; but You kept me!

Yours truly,

A child of the King

Vanessa Ray

My Prayer

I decree and declare that by Your stripes, I am healed from the crown of my head to the soul of my feet. I will prosper and be in good health even as my soul prosper, in Jesus name, Amen!

INTRODUCTION

Welcome to a life of struggles, disappointments, and accomplishments! Life brings about circumstances and situations that you can't begin to imagine. You have to hold onto God's unchanging hand. He will never put more on you than you can bear. You have to be strong and courageous; stay focused, and never give up on your dreams. Just know that God is the only one that you can depend on. He is Alpha, Omega, the Beginning, and the End. Trials and tribulations come to make you strong, but you have to endure until the end. No matter what it may look like or how bad it may seem, have faith and praise your way through. Prayer does change things. The Lord is my strength. I hope you will be blessed by this book. Just know you can make it if you try! Don't give up…...the test comes only to make you strong. Trouble don't last always.

Some of My Favorite Scriptures

Proverbs 3:5,6 (KJV)

Trust in the Lord with all thine heart; and lean not unto thine own understanding. In all thy ways acknowledge him, and he shall direct thy paths.

Matthew 6:33 (KJV)

But seek ye first the kingdom of God and his righteousness; and all these things shall be added unto you.

Ephesians 6:10-13 (KJV)

Finally, my brethren, be strong in the Lord, and in the power of his might. Put on the whole armour of God, that ye may be able to stand against the wiles of the devil. For we wrestle not against flesh and blood, but against principalities, against powers, against the rulers of the darkness of this world, against spiritual wickedness in high places. Wherefore take unto you the whole armour of God, that ye may be able to withstand in the evil day, and having done all, to stand.

-1-

A MOTHERLESS AND FATHERLESS CHILD

-1-

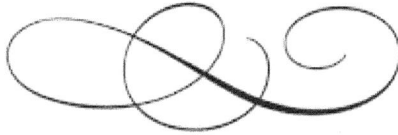

A Motherless and Fatherless Child

As far back as I can remember, I was 5 years old. My sister was 4, and my brother 6. My mom walked us to my grandmother's house and just left us there without an explanation. Someday I knew she would come back to get me, but she never did. Over a period of months...then years...she would pop up for a few days, then would leave again for a long period of time. When she came, I just knew *that* time would be the one time she would take me with her but she didn't...only to leave me heartbroken yet again. She would always say "I will be back to get you", so I held onto that promise until the next time I saw her. She would always bring me stuff when she would come home. My sister and brother resented her because they didn't have much to do with her. I had a love for her that was unconditional. As for my dad, he left and moved out of town for work. I vividly remember us being a family at one time. Growing up, we didn't have much.

My grandmother had 11 kids she was raising on her own, and we lived in the projects. Money was short, and times were really hard; but she did the best she knew how. There were no birthday parties or Christmas celebrations that I can recall. Yet, somehow I always managed to see the positive side of things and made the best out of the situations because, eventually, I knew things had to get better. I can remember something that stuck with me at one point in time. We were a family...my mother and father had a house together on Hurst street and they loved us.

My sister, brother and I were not shown much love growing up; but somehow I have a lot of love in my heart despite the way I was raised. Let me fast-forward to when I was a young teen, about 14 years old. I worked as an after-school babysitter for one of my teachers at her home On the weekends, she was really nice to me. She would always give me chips and cookies that she would buy off this truck that came through the community where she lived.   The cookies and chips were very good!   I can remember the truck was tan. I just knew that when he came through, I was going to get some treats. I enjoyed working for her and I really needed the money.

I also made hair bows in my spare time. My aunt would take them to work and sell them for me. Also, in middle school, I learned how to sew. I would make things and sell them to people. I set up a snack shop at my grandmother's house where I would sell snacks to the neighborhood kids; so I guess you can say I have always been an entrepreneur because I was always thinking of ways to earn money. I made Christmas shirts, socks, and all types of jewelry to sell so that I could provide for myself. The sewing class went on through high school. I learned how to visualize things, sketch them down on paper, and make my own patterns for the garments I created. Sewing is my first passion!

My Dad

My Mom

-2-

FEELING CONFUSED AND LOST

-2-

Feeling Confused and Lost

I was in high school, specifically the 9th grade, when I became pregnant with my first child. Growing up, I wasn't taught about the *birds and the bees*, or about sex in my home. Anything I learned was from friends, and whatever the school was allowed to teach us. So when I became pregnant, I wasn't scared. I felt like I would finally have someone to love and my child would love me back unconditionally, the one thing I was missing!!

The ability to love was very important to me. When I had my daughter, she brought so much joy to my life. I gave her all of my love. Times were hard; so with the money I had earned, I bought material and made me and her some clothing. I was assigned to the alternative school for pregnant teens until I gave birth to my daughter. Afterwards, I could return to my high school. I didn't quit, drop out, or get behind on my classes. I had determined that I was going to successfully finish school no matter what!

I had always wanted a better life for myself...especially now that I had a child who I am responsible for, and I wasn't married at the time. I had many sleepless days and nights, but I pressed my way through in spite of my situation and all of the negative things people would say about me. Every summer, I would work on the Cedar program that would employ low income kids and pay them an hourly wage. That's how I would provide for me and my daughter.

.

-3-

PUTTING THINGS IN PERSPECTIVE

-3-

Putting Things in Perspective

When I was in the 11th grade, things were seeming to get a little better. I was one year closer to graduating from high school, and a guy from the senior class asked me to go with him to the prom. It made me feel important. With the money I earned from working, I bought some fabric so that I could make my own prom dress. The dress was peach, and made out of satin material. When I finished, I was so proud of that dress. It made me look and feel like a princess; and for the first time, I felt like somebody important. At the church I attended, the Pastor and members would always say to me, "you are somebody and God loves you!" I heard them at the time, but I didn't feel that way. I wasn't raised to go to church, or even taken to church. I made that decision on my own. I just knew that if there was a God, I needed and wanted Him in my life...if it would make things better for me.

I was a teenager and I didn't enjoy my life at all. I was wondering why no one loved me? What did I do to feel so abandoned and alone?? I don't ever remember hearing the words "I love you" or "I am proud of you". I just knew I wanted to be different and live a better life than the one I had experienced growing up as a child. I never had my own bedroom, and was never thrown a birthday party. I do remember my dad coming to visit, and he had a lot of toys and clothing for us; but somehow that wasn't enough. I felt a void in my life. When he left, it would be a while before we would see him again. My brother and I wanted to go live with him, which eventually we did thinking our lives would be better if we had at least one **stable** parent...only to end up back at the place that was familiar to us...home...and back at my old high school.

Prom Dress

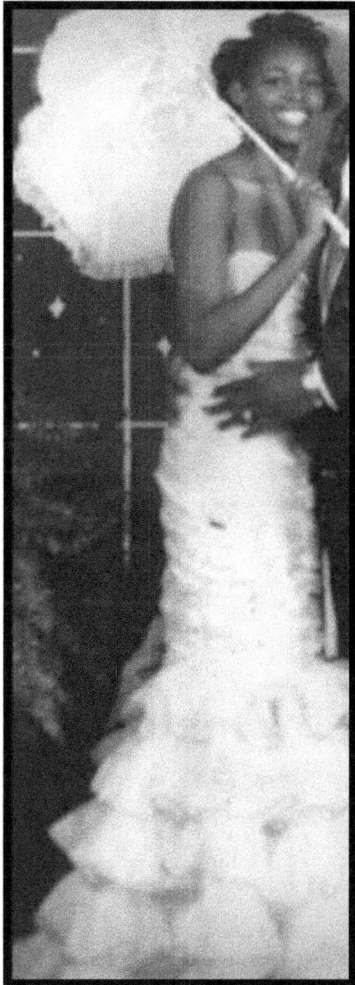

-4-

FEELING DETERMINED

-4-

Feeling Determined

A s a senior in high school, I tried out for basketball, color guard, pageants, and was a cheerleader for the Rec League. Our team color was orange and white. I was in FHA and sung with the choir. I had determined that I was going to make it somehow. I had always wanted to attend college, and I knew I was going to need a scholarship to pay for it. So I was attempting to get into any organization that would offer a scholarship. Little did I know, I could apply for a Pell grant. It was that time again...senior prom...so I took my same date from my 11th grade year. As I was preparing to graduate, I became frightened because I didn't know what I was going to do. I had nothing to be a part of anymore. Life begins after you graduate from high school. I was excited that I made it! I was graduating despite the chaos in my life! When I walked across the stage, I had no one but myself. No mother, no father, no family members. Just me, myself, and I to celebrate one of the biggest achievements in my life!

Again, I was glad that I made it in spite of my obstacles. I didn't become a statistic—a high school dropout with a baby. I was proud of myself!! I didn't go straight to college after graduation. I just worked while I was on the work program at one of the facilities where I worked during the summer. They liked my work ethics and offered me a job, so I accepted and worked as a clerk in the child support division.

FHA/HERC

FHA

Senior Portrait

Vanessa Ray

-5-

THINGS WERE LOOKING A LITTLE BETTER

-5-

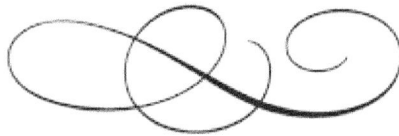

Things Were Looking a Little Better

When I turned 19, I became pregnant with twins. I was living in my own place; my daughter Brittany had her own room, so things started looking a little better. My mom came to live with me. I felt good because I knew she didn't have to go from place to place or be in the streets. I stayed sick a lot. I was in and out of the hospital because the doctor didn't want me to give birth to my twins too early.

Things were going well between me and my kids' dad.   Then, on January 20, 1990, I gave birth to my twin daughters.   My mom was there for me the whole time.   When I gave birth to them, one of them was sick.   She had too many white blood cells, and my blood pressure stayed high for about 3 days.   As a result, I wasn't able to see her until the day before I was being released.   The doctor didn't want me up because he didn't want me to have a seizure.   Back then, there was no FaceTime.

Only a few people had cell phones or cameras; so therefore I would ask my mom and the people who had seen my daughter what she looked like...and are they identical twins.   I think that's probably why I can tell them apart.   On the 4th day, they said that if my blood pressure was down, they would let me go home.   You should have seen me eating ice and putting a cool towel on my head!!   My babies and I were doing well enough to go home, so I was super excited!   When the doctor came in, everything looked good and we were released.   That's when fear kicked in.   I thought about the fact that I now have a 3 year old **and two** infant babies. I had a lot of questions, like "how do I feed them at the same time, how do I change them, how do I bathe them?" I was just confused. I thank God for my mother. She really took good care of my girls. At times, when I would be sleeping and they start crying, my mother would have already fed one and taking care of the other. She really loved and cherish those girls. She would promise to me that she was going to buy them a double stroller. She didn't have a job at the time, nor do I remember her ever having one. But she got them that double stroller! She was one proud grandmother.

One day, she left me there with the kids by myself. I asked her if she could help me get them to sleep before she left. She did, but they awakened before she returned. They were both hungry and crying, so I had to be super mom and figure out how I was going to feed these 2 week old babies at the same time. I thought that maybe I could prop them up with the bottle, but there were barely opening their eyes and couldn't lift up their heads. So, I don't know how I did it, but I put one in my arm and the other in the other arm, held the bottle in both hands, and fed my babies. When they were done feeding, I laid both of them across my legs and burped them. Afterwards, they drifted back to sleep. I felt like a conqueror! Like I had passed a test. But I was so glad when my mom returned. I shared that story with her. She laughed, but told me that I did a good job.

My Twins

-6-

IF ONLY I KNEW

-6-

If Only I Knew

Shayla and Tarayla were about 3 weeks old, and Brittany had just turned 4. I had just finished giving them a bath and putting them to bed. I was getting ready to take a shower. I had the window up in the bedroom, letting the breeze come in. As some may know, it gets very hot in the project building. As I was getting ready to let the window down, I noticed a black van, some detective cars, and the police pulling up.

Just as I closed the window, I heard a loud boom. As I turned around to go downstairs, I saw men dressed in all black with guns pointed at me, telling me to get down! So I walked in the room and laid across the bed. I was so scared and wondering what was going on. One of the men handcuffed me and allowed me to sit up on the bed. He started questioning me, asked me questions like "are there any drugs in here?" I told him no, and that I have a child in the other room. I asked him if I could go get her, so he guided me in there to get her. She was too young to know what was going on.

The gentleman asked me about the whereabouts of my kids' father, and I said that I didn't know and that he was not here. So he told me that he was going to bring the search dog upstairs to see if any drugs were present. When I asked him what was going on downstairs, he told me that he would explain that to me later. He ensured me that they didn't really want me. They wanted my kids' father. Of course they knew his name already. The detective said that if they can't get him, the will take me because it was my house. By that time, the social worker had made it there to take my kids. I heard my family outside screaming and yelling. Some were even crying, trying to figure out what was going on. So what do you know...my kids' father shows up! I was told that if I had someone who could take my kids, they would release my kids to them. So my kids' aunt took them for me. The detectives told me that if my kids' father lets them know that I had nothing to do with what was going on, they wouldn't take me to jail.

Who would've guessed that my high school sweetheart, the love of my life, and the father of my 3 weeks old kids, would let me go to jail for something he knew I had nothing to do with?! True...I knew he sold drugs. I had even counted some of the money myself. But I didn't sell any drugs, and didn't allow him to bring the drugs to my house...at least I though I made that very clear. I was very devastated, scared, and still sick from giving birth to my twins. I just knew that he wasn't going to allow me to go to jail. Well...he did, and I had to stay there for 3 days, or 72 hours. That was my first time in jail. I thought that I was going to die and couldn't make it in there. I remember asking the detective if being in jail was like they show it on TV. He told me no, it's not like that. I broke down crying. He really felt bad for me. He told me that they were going to try to talk to my kids' father so that I can go home to my kids.

When they took me to the back, I knew my life was over! But what do you know...my mom's best friend Sarah was in the for the weekend. I promise you...I knew then that God was looking out for me. What seemed to be the worst part of my life, He put Sarah there to help me get through this. I'm telling you, she made sure I was good and really did look out for me, and got the things I needed. The detectives came and got me out of my cell to ask me some questions. My kids' father had sent word by one of the prisoners telling me to not say anything. Well, that went in one ear and out the other!

Picture of me

-7-

THE TURNAROUND

-7-

The Turnaround

The 72 hours were up. We were going to be transported to the Lee County Justice Center...so they told us. But once they put me and my kids' father in the police car together, they said we were going to Montgomery to the federal prison. I was numb. I started talking to him, telling him that he know I had nothing to do with this; and that I will tell anything I can and know so that I can get back to my kids. I told him that it was obvious to me at that point that he couldn't love me like he said he did, or he wouldn't have let me go through this. So upon arriving to the jail waiting to be taking to the prison, we had to go before the judge for a preliminary hearing. The judge told me that when it is time for sentencing, he is going to give me the same sentence that he is going to give to my kids' father. I broke down and told the kids' father that I hated him. The judge sent him to federal prison with no bond.

With the little I did know about the Lord, I asked Him to please help me. The only thing I could think about were my kids. When I went before the judge, he told me that they knew I had nothing to do with this situation. He informed me that I will be charged, but he allowed me to sign my own bond...and the detectives will take me back home to my kids. The judge warned me to not discuss anything with the detectives because it can be used against me. As they were taking me back to my kids, the only thing I was doing was thanking God and crying! They only asked me for the address.

When I got out of the car, I ran in the house and laid across my kids where they were sleeping and just cried and cried. When I was able to pull myself together, I needed to go back to my house to see what was still there, and see the damage. Of course, I got evicted from my home and had to live with my ex-boyfriend's parents for a little while. That didn't last long. The grandfather helped me get another place. I used to walk around with my head down. I was at my lowest point in my life. At the place where I lived, this old lady would always be outside. I really didn't know she was paying me any attention.

Everyone had a lot to say about my situation, so I thought she was just one of those people. So one day when I was outside, she said "baby, come here." I went over and she said "I want you to pick your head up and get that look off your face and act like you are somebody! We all know what happened to you wasn't your fault." She gave me the confidence I needed to pick up the pieces and try to make a life for me and my kids. Things were really hard for me. I felt like no one loved, or even cared about me. At that point,

I didn't trust anyone. I knew of God and a few scriptures from the church I attended, Bethel #1 Baptist Church.

Romans 8:28 (KJV)

And we know that all things work together for good to them that love God, to them who are the called according to His purpose.

-8-

BOUNCING BACK & THEN A SETBACK

-8-

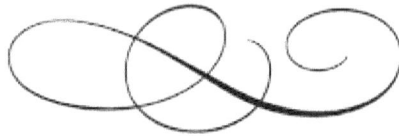

Bouncing Back, & Then a Setback

I started working at Diversified Products, known as DP, on third shift. I had a mobile home and lived on Alabama Street. My mom came over and asked if she could live with me. I told her yes. She asked if Jack could stay there too, and I told her no. I didn't care much for him. He was very controlling and abusive to my mom. She had been drinking. She got mad at me and cursed me out for saying that her boyfriend could not live in my house. I just took it because when she was drunk, that was just what she did. I knew she didn't mean it and she would be okay when she sobered up for a day or 2...whenever that would be! She was an alcoholic. I became pregnant with my 4th child, and I hadn't heard from or seen my mom in a while. I knew she would just pop up because that's just what she did...pop in for a while, then back out for months at a time. But this seem extremely longer than usual. But I didn't ask any questions.

So out of the blue, my grandmother (her mom) called and suggested that I put out a police report on my mom because they thought she was missing. Well, she hung out with one of my aunts, which was her drinking buddy. I guess she told them something. I asked them how long had they known, and she said that she didn't know and my aunt just had told them. So I went and talked to my aunt and asked her why she thought my mom was missing. After she explained to me why, I went and put of the police report on my mom. I remember...it was in the summer of 1990 and the heat index was like 110 degrees. It was a very hot summer! Once I filed the report, we received all kinds of calls of what people thought they knew of my mom's whereabouts. None of it was true. Her so-called boyfriend was acting really strange. The investigation went on for months. The police were finding bodies everywhere that year. One day, a knock came at my door. I answered the door. It was the lead detective assigned to my mom's case, along with his assistant. They stopped by to ask me a few more questions, like did my mom have any broken bones or dental records. I said yes.

I knew because I witnessed her being abused a lot. One time a man stomped on her, breaking her arm and knocking out her teeth. I saw her eyes being blackened shut, her being locked into a house while her husband beat her, and cut her breast. So yeah, I knew. After the lead detective finished with all the questions, they left the house. Then I heard another knock on the door a few minutes later. I answered the door and it was them again. I asked them was anything wrong? He answered and said yes. He said "I don't know how to tell you this, but we found a body and we are pretty sure it's your mom, so you may want to tell your family." I just passed out screaming and crying. They consoled me until I was able to get myself together. I never knew that the day my mom cursed me out would be my last day ever seeing or talking to her again. I would always tell her that I love her no matter what she would say to me.

I didn't have any guilt in my heart. I just wish I would have allowed her boyfriend to come and stay. Maybe things would have been different. Maybe that was her cry for help. Be careful how you treat people, and what you say to hurt them. It just may be your last chance, then it is too late. I carried that "what if" around with me for years and years.

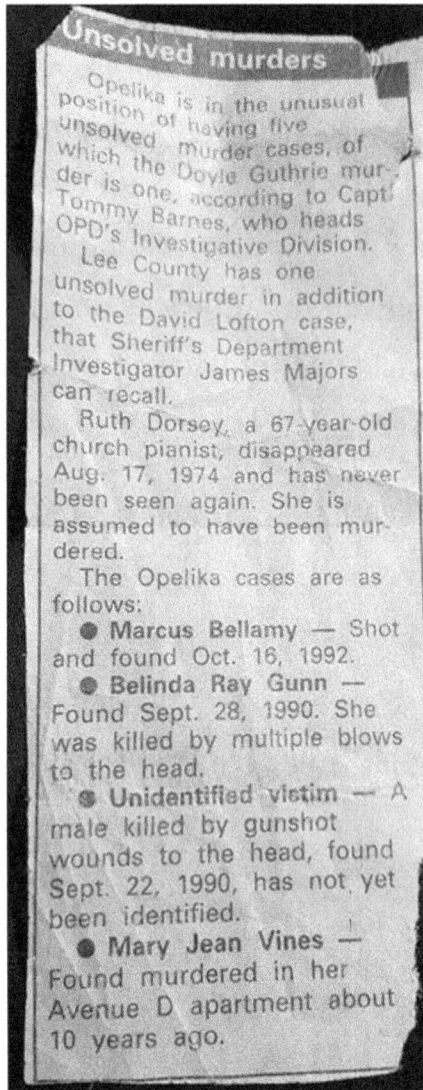

Unsolved murders

Opelika is in the unusual position of having five unsolved murder cases, of which the Doyle Guthrie murder is one, according to Capt. Tommy Barnes, who heads OPD's Investigative Division.

Lee County has one unsolved murder in addition to the David Lofton case, that Sheriff's Department Investigator James Majors can recall.

Ruth Dorsey, a 67-year-old church pianist, disappeared Aug. 17, 1974 and has never been seen again. She is assumed to have been murdered.

The Opelika cases are as follows:

● **Marcus Bellamy** — Shot and found Oct. 16, 1992.

● **Belinda Ray Gunn** — Found Sept. 28, 1990. She was killed by multiple blows to the head.

● **Unidentified victim** — A male killed by gunshot wounds to the head, found Sept. 22, 1990, has not yet been identified.

● **Mary Jean Vines** — Found murdered in her Avenue D apartment about 10 years ago.

Article about mom

-9-

THE PAIN AND GRIEVING

-9-

The Pain and Grieving

The process to determine if the body they found was her was the longest and most devastating part of my life. All of my mom's kids, brothers, and sisters had to have blood drawn more than one time because the previous blood they drew would spoil. So the wait felt like a lifetime. In the meanwhile, the detective was questioning people who names were brought up around the time she became missing. He brought me the article of clothing that was on her body. I was scared. I didn't know what was in the brown paper bag. When I stopped shaking and built up my nerves, I was able to look at them. He had a bra, a pair of khaki pants, and a red shirt tied up in the front. I knew instantly they were hers. I broke down crying. The detective informed me the autopsy still had to be performed, and they can even use dried blood. He also let me know that he had picked up a suspect, which was her boyfriend at the time, and was going to try to perform a polygraph test on him.

So a few months went by. I stayed in contact with the detective. He would keep me updated by telling me about some leads he had. He even warned me about some suspicions he had about one person, but didn't have enough evidence to prove anything. So time went by and I needed to just get away from everything. I went out of town for a few days and returned home on a Sunday. I grabbed a newspaper to read, and what do you know...there was an article in there about my mom. I read it only to find out that the state was ordered to bury the Jane Doe (which now has a name—my mother Belinda Ann Ray-Gunn) was buried under plot #71 in Evergreen Cemetery. I went to the police station so fast! I talked to the detective that was on the case. He explained to me that the state said my mom was taking up taxpayer money by continuing to hold the decomposed body. He said that he tried to contact me. Well, my number didn't change! I asked him, "what if that had been your mother? Would you have wanted to read about her burial in the newspaper??" He said that I could have her dug up and have a funeral for her. My mind just went blank. I didn't know what to do, so I just left and went to the cemetery where she was buried.

There was a yard stick in the ground with her name on it. I was thinking, how could they just do that to her? It was like she walked off the face of the earth and no one cared. I was pregnant with my 4th child still. I went into a state of depression. I just didn't want to live anymore. The way my mother was treated hurt me to the core of my soul. She is my mother and I loved her dearly in spite of who she was and what she did. She was my best friend. When she was sober, she was as good as gold, and would do anything for you and give you her last. She was the best cook. I loved her personality. It's just that when she drank, she was another person, as if she hated herself. I remember when she tried to jump in a well and kill herself. She had overdosed on pills. I just couldn't understand what was going on in her life that made her not want to live anymore. I spent many years of my life wondering if she would pop up again, or if she was somewhere and didn't know who she was. When I went to another city, I was always hoping she would be there. I saw many faces that I wanted to be her, but it never was. I didn't get the closure that I needed.

I dreamed about her quite often. I just couldn't let go. I also carried what I thought was hate; but a strong dislike in my heart towards the man suspected of killing her, but couldn't find enough evidence to prove it. I ran across him in a grocery store one day. I approached him in rage and told him that I know he killed my mother, and that he could have laid her on my doorstep so that I could have seen her body, and the he didn't have to do her like that! I also warned him that he will suffer for what he did to my mom, even if it is on his dying bed. I started hitting him. My grandmother grabbed me and calmed me down. I just wanted him to hurt like I was hurting. He walked around and got away with murdering my mother. A polygraph test couldn't be performed on him because he was an alcoholic. The test would be determined as inconclusive, and they didn't have enough evidence to prove it. But everything was pointed at him and he was the last one seen with her. Plus, he was very abusive to her. I would hear him say to her that if he can't have her, no one can. I guess he made sure of that.

Mom

-10-

MOVING FORWARD

-10-

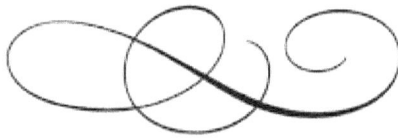

Moving Forward

A few years later, I attended Southern Union Community College for Cosmetology. I was starting to fulfill my college dreams, even though I had 4 kids at the time. But I wasn't going to let that stop me. I was really enjoying it, but things got really hard for me trying to juggle school, work, and being a mother. So I decided to put school on the backburner for a while. I continued to work, and braided hair on the side.

Things were getting better for me and my girls. We had finally gotten some stability. I purchased my first car, a green Mazda Protégé, and the bank financed it. I remember, it was brand new, a 1993 model with no miles on it. I was working at the Justice Center. After a few years there, I began to realize that office work just wasn't for me. So I resigned and started doing work as a manufacturer. I started hanging out a little bit on the weekends when the kids went with their grandparents. I began to feel confident within myself. I moved into a mobile home I was purchasing. I became pregnant with my 5th child. I was working at Diversified Products.

I was about five months pregnant at the time when I went to work one early morning around 7am. As I proceeded to start working, I heard one of my coworkers talking really loud as she was walking up and down the line. I was informed that she was talking to me, so I started to pay attention to her. She asked me what was I looking at, and I said, "excuse me, are you referring to me?" She said, "yes, I am talking to you." I informed the supervisor what was going on. He took a seat on a bucket and said she isn't going to do anything. However, she came to my work area using profanity, and saying that they are going to find me dead like they found my momma. Immediately, everything went black! I started hitting, punching, kicking, and pulling her hair. I was in a range! It brought up so many emotions and opened up old wounds. The employees pulled us apart. I was so hurt and angry. I got fired that day. I was only going to work there for a few more weeks anyway, but I never imagined anything like that happening. I totally shut down once more. I trusted this person with this information and she used it against me.

A few months later, I gave birth to my baby girl Nidica Ray. I had 5 girls with no husband. I was a single mom. I really needed to do some soul searching and figure out what I wanted to do with my life, and continuing to have babies wasn't the answer. I got a job at Friskars working 2nd shift. Soon after, I got promoted to shift leader and started working 1st shift, but I felt something was missing. One night when I got home from work, I had decided to take a drive to clear my mind. And what do you know, I had an accident. It was pitch black dark, and I was coming around a curve when a man ran the stop sign and hit me head-on. The impact was so hard, my face hit the steering wheel and I blacked out. I can remember hearing a voice telling me to stay woke, don't leave....and shaking me telling me to stay woke. I was blacking in and out. It was one of my classmates who now owns a funeral home. I feel like my classmate saved my life, for had I fallen asleep, I could have slipped into a coma. When I arrived at the hospital in the ambulance, all of my family members were there. News really travel fast, I thought.

My mouth was shifted, my face was swollen really big, and my teeth had broken off in my gum. I only stayed for a few days, then released. Nothing could be done until the swelling went down. I was going to need surgery. While I was down, I saw my life flash before my eyes. I didn't want to die and leave my kids without their mother. It was time for me to have surgery. The doctor informed me that if my jaw was broken, they would need to wire my mouth shut and I would have to eat through a straw. At that time, I was already consuming liquids only. I was praying that my jaw wasn't broken, but I wouldn't know until I woke up from surgery. Thank you Lord it wasn't broken! The doctor only had to remove the broken teeth.

My Daughter Nidica

-11-

TRYING TO FILL THE VOID

-11-

Trying to Fill the Void

While I was in the process of recovering, I had time to think about a lot of things. It took about 1 month for me to start feeling normal again. Swelling was completely gone and I returned to work only to feel like it was a void there. So after contemplating, I just decided that I wanted to go somewhere else and make a fresh new start. I had some experience in being a server, so I

I asked for the manager and told her that I was moving there after my kids got out for the summer. She said she would hold the job for me until May 27, 2001; and if I wasn't there, she would give the job to someone else. When my kids got out of school for the summer, I packed all my stuff, put it in storage, and only took what we needed. I hand no home to go to. I had a full tank of gas and enough money for only one night's stay at the hotel. We stopped at a hotel in Marietta, which cost $37. I was to report to work at 11 pm that night. My oldest daughter, who was 15 at the time, stayed there with the other kids until I got off.

When I went into work, I was going to be a server; but she was shorthanded in having a hostess and asked if I could do it. I said that I could, but I told her that I really needed to be a server that night. She didn't know my situation so I explained a little of it to her. So she switched some people around because I didn't have any plans at all and I was out of money. So it worked in my

I would go down and feed my girls. The lady running the kitchen would always give me extra food to take back to the room for the girls. I would bring food home from work when I could. We were in the hotel about a month when my boss informed me that the apartment complex she lived was taking 10 canned goods as a deposit and move-in special. I just knew that couldn't be true, but I went by there anyway and it was very true! So I filled out an application and gave my 10 canned goods. Within a week, we were moving in a gated community off of Franklin Road.

I was sure things were looking up for me and my girls. I sent them back home for the summer until I could get some beds and other furniture for them. The church helped me out with a lot of things. I also got a second job at a department store. Since the girls were not there at the time, I could work until it was time for school to start there. I started applying for different jobs so that I could be able to provide for my girls when they came a job as customer service team leader. I accepted it, and it was a 9am to 5pm shift. They said favor isn't fair, but it is good to have! It had been people working there for years; and I got offered the position with little experience. I was so proud of that job. I got some good incentives like free tickets to the Braves game in the Lexus level with VIP treatment. The summer was coming to an end. I got off of work one day to head to Alabama to get my kids. As I got out of the parking deck headed toward the light, I had an accident. A van ran the red light and hit me head-on.

My seatbelt locked me in, cutting across my chest. I had a hard time breathing. Some of my coworkers saw that it was me and came over to help. They thought I was dead, but I was pinned down in the car. They didn't move me and they stayed with me until the paramedics arrived. My boss had some of my family members' phone numbers, so she contacted them. My uncles and aunts came to Emory Hospital where I was admitted.

Me and Briel

Brittany and Nidica

-12-

RECOVERING AND RETURNING
BACK HOME

-12-

Recovering and Returning Back Home

While at my grandmother's house, my eyes were opened to a lot of things. I had seen my life flashed before my eyes for a second time. I didn't know if God was trying to tell me something, or what was going on! I was so scared, wondering what if I would have died, how was anyone going to know I had no family in Marietta. A big but something was still missing. I had to do physical therapy there 3 times a week. I was at work and heard about what happened on 9/11. Of course being in Atlanta working in a high rise building, they sent everyone home. The whole country was on alert. Once again, fear crept in. So I decided I was going to just go back home and try to make a life there for me and my kids. One thing I did know was I could always go home. I contacted the Auburn housing authority to see if they had any Section 8 or public housing available. The lady I talked to told me that something would be available soon, so I applied. When she called me for the interview, she gave me a 3 bedroom apartment for me and my girls. So I moved back home in 2003.

I didn't start working immediately. I was trying to see what did I really want to do with my life as far as career-wise.. So I started seeing what I was good at, or would enjoy doing. I was watching TV one day, and Rivertown School of Beauty came across the screen. I me to come and meet with them, and I did. So I enrolled in the Nail Technician program, which was about 6 to 8 months long. By then, I was 33 years old with 5 kids, no job, and living in the projects; but with a determined spirit, I just knew it was more to life than the cards I had been dealt. So I started school and everything was going well. I started working part-time while going to school. A few months in school, things took a turn for the worst. I had a third car accident. This one was the worst one! One guy hit us from behind just as we were approaching an overpass bridge. The SUV spun around several times.

The only thing I could do was to pray. I saw that we were about to fall over the bridge. Just so happen that a guard rail was there. I was pinned in on my side. Nidica and Brittany were also in the truck with me. We had went to pick up a puppy that we named Denali, a shih tzu. Nidica had a really bad concussion. Brittany was just shaken up. She held on to that puppy for dear life. I had whiplash. My back and my leg were hurt. When we were in the 23 years he had been doing this, he had never had to transport a dog to the hospital. We were all treated and released. A few days passed, I had to go back to the hospital. Back at home, I couldn't walk without experiencing a lot of pain. I couldn't go back to work and Nidica was having some head issues as well. Things were just horrible. I needed care, and so did my baby. She had a little memory loss. She didn't pass the 1st grade because she couldn't remember what was being taught. I had to have intense physical therapy. I know I needed the Lord to help me.

Depression was beginning to set in. I felt worthless, unlovable, and like I didn't have any purpose. The devil was trying to take me out. I didn't have any fight in me left. I remember laying there in bed and watching TV. This church program came on. It was a local church in the area, so I decided that when Sunday came, my kids and I were going to attend.

Nail Technician diploma

Rivertown School of Beauty, Barber,Skin Care & Nails

Diploma

Presented to:

Vanessa Brooks

For the completion of the course of

Nail Technician

This 15th day of December, 2004

Jan Cookman, Director

-13-

NEW LEASE ON LIFE

-13-

New Lease on Life

Sunday came, and I attended the church. The Pastor gave me a word and I took it to heart and started doing some soul searching. I returned back to school to finish the nail technician program. I was more focused than ever. I entered a contest to work for this nail art company in Las Vegas. They were going to select 100 people. Thousands art and send it in. I had to wait about 4 to 6 weeks to hear anything from them. Another student in my class entered also. I was patiently waiting, checking the mail every day. So one day after class, I went home and a letter was in the mail from them addressed to me. I was so nervous, I prayed before I opened the letter. I was opening it little by little. So finally I got it opened. Most letters start off by saying something like "I would like to inform you…" I was already feeling rejected; just felt like I couldn't get any good breaks. Well, to my surprise, I had been chosen to fly out to Las Vegas for training.

Overwhelmed with joy, I couldn't wait to go to school the next day to share this good news with my class and instructor. I got in class and shared the good news. The other student shared hers too. We were both chosen. The owner of the school and the other students were so proud of us, and congratulating us. I felt like a celebrity. The other student and I were flown to Las Vegas with all expenses paid. We stayed at the upper to be treated as such. The owner of the company took really good care of us. Life was beginning to feel great for me. The company flew me out once or twice a month for the weekend to work at the Premier Nail shows. When I was in Austin, Texas, I was selected for an appearance in the Nail Pro Magazine in the August 2004 issue...which I am in. My nail career was taking off full force while I was still in school. I competed in the Nail Pro Competition at the Cobb Galleria in Atlanta, GA in 2004. I graduated with a grade of 98 in the course.

My instructor thought I had some previous experience in nails since I caught on so quickly. But it was God who blessed me with my many talents and the know-how to do things that I had never done. I remember when I got my first job as a nail technician. I was so excited! It was very different from being in school. I found out that I still needed to learn more and more because there was always something new coming out. I had to keep up with the new trend. I stayed focus because I knew someday I knew someday I wanted to be a sole proprietor entrepreneur. I worked at a few shops along the way, but I really enjoyed the spa atmosphere. It was calming and relaxing. I also learned how I wanted to run my shop and what kind of employees I wanted. I had some type of experiences in this industry.

Graduation Picture

-14-

BECOMING A BUSINESS OWNER
AND ENTREPRENEUR

-14-

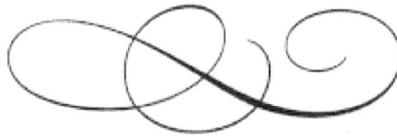

Becoming a Business Owner and Entrepreneur

I n 2008, I decided that I was going to step out on faith and open up my own business. I didn't have anyone to guide me. I just did it. I found a building in where I thought was a good location. I named it "Nuyounique Nails". I was a proud woman. It was located in Auburn, AL. My daughter Nidica helped me design the shop. She drew art on the walls. It was a and newspaper ads. I had some people from the church I attended who supported me. They were faithful clients whom I really appreciated. I worked in the shop alone. I wasn't sure if I wanted any employees that time because I was just starting out, learning as I went. Things were going well. I decided to go back to school to get my Nail Technician Instructor license. The course was 250 credit hours. I didn't know what I was thinking! Being my own boss and going to school was a little hectic. I had to learn how to juggle the two. I did a lot of praying because if the on thing I know is that prayer works and changes things.

I attended the same school where I earned my Nail Tech degree. Things were overwhelming for me. I ended up in the hospital for a few days. I thought I was having a heart attack because my chest was tightening up and I was short of breath. So the lady that worked two doors down from me gave me some Bayer aspirin and drove me whatever it is, you need to let it go before it kills you! He admitted me into the hospital so they could watch me for a few days, and so that I could also get some rest. I didn't rest very well because I was scared and confused. I thought once again the devil was trying to take me out. I thought about this saying I knew: *"the devil had literally peeped into my future and seen how the Lord was about to bless me."* I do know the Lord does things to get our attention too. School was stressful at the time. I was approaching 40 years of age. I didn't have the mind of a 20 year old...trying to consume all of that information, run a business, and be a mother was taking a toll on my body.

I had to commute 40 minutes there and 40 back. It was in a different time zone, so I would lose an hour. I went 4 days a week from 9am-4pm and ran my business the other days. Plus I worked part time in the evenings after I left the shop. I didn't get a loan to open my shop. I used my own money to fund it. It took me four months to the Nail Technician program. I accepted it and decided to close the shop. I needed a steady paycheck. I thought making that decision was the best one for me. I enjoyed teaching. It was awesome. I say about 2 months into teaching, I learned how to do lesson planning and how to run the program. Things ran smoothly. I had a class as large as 26 adult students, which was challenging. The ages ranged from 18-50 years old. Therefore, I had to be counselor, parent, advisor, and teacher. I thought I had some life issues! You can never tell what a person is going through by just looking at them. I am so glad I had the Lord on my side to help me get through this.

My faith was strong, I knew how to pray, and I was saved. I don't know if I could have been able to handle all of that. I have a tendency to carry other people's weight around with me as if the problem was mine. I am very compassionate and tenderhearted when it comes to people. Every student I had that completed the program went and passed the state board. I was one proud so I wanted to give it a try again. When my last student graduated in 2010, I resigned and opened up a nail salon in Phenix City, AL. I named it, *Diva's & Gent's Nailz Lounge.* I employed 4 nail techs and 2 hairstylists. I had a boutique up front and a snack shop. It was a one-stop shop. A few of my students came to work with me. It was beautiful inside. The décor was read, black, and white. The students were working off commission. Some did booth rent. The hairstylists did booth rental. When you are in this business, it takes time to build clientele. You have to be dedicated and committed. Advertising and networking are a plus. You have to put in some long hours and a lot of time. I stayed there for a little over a year.

Instructor Diploma

Rivertown School of Beauty, Barber, Skin Care & Nails

Diploma

Presented to:

Vanessa Brooks

For the completion of the course of

Nail Technician Instructor

Granted on this the 5th day of June, 2009:

_____
Jennifer Jones, Director

-15-

TRANSITIONING

-15-

Transitioning

I decided to move my business home to Opelika, AL in 2011. It was located near the bus station. I had a receptionist, hairstylist, braider, makeup artist, and nail technician. I had the banker personally come meet me about my business needs. I thought maybe they had something to contribute to help me get started, but that wasn't the case. She did help steer me in the right direction and gave me some helpful would be great since I knew a lot of people there. I learned quickly that some people don't want to support you because they think you will be doing better than them. It's a shame we don't want to support a person's business because of jealousy and envy. I believe in supporting people with their dreams. You never know how that may inspire someone, or that someone can help you pursue your dream. It is very challenging being an entrepreneur. Sometimes you win, sometimes you lose; but you gotta keep trying. Don't give up! How would you know if you don't try.

I remember reading "if you can make a dollar, you can make a million dollars." Well, I am going for mine and I hope to take a few people along with me. Things were rough for me. I always took what little I had and tried to make it work. I was doing this on my own with my own money. I didn't save up for a business or take out a loan. I worked another job while trying to build my business.

oh Lord, enlarge my territory and bless me indeed. The location of my shop had turned out to not be so good for my type of business, so I moved to another spot in Opelika. It was a nice and cozy place. This time, I decided to work alone.

I only lived a few blocks away from my shop. I had an ATM inside my shop, and things were going good. I had started dating someone, business was good, and my family was doing well. I was expecting my 2nd grandbaby. Jordan North is my first grandson. I had some new business ventures that I was working on. I was hosting handbag parties, jewelry parties, and networking events at the shop, which were a success. About six months had passed, and then I was hit with another blow!

Grandson

-16-

I THOUGHT MY HEART COULDN'T
TAKE ANYMORE

-16-

I Thought My Heart Couldn't Take Anymore

My daughter gave birth to a baby girl. Her name is Ja'Laya Matteria Butler. I fell in love all over again. She was so beautiful...and still is...and she loves her nana. When she came home from the hospital, she and her mother lived with me. One day, Ja'Layla's dad came over to sit with them so I could run some errands. When I returned *my life right, go back to school, and join the military so I can take care of my daughter.* I encouraged him and told him he can do it and don't let anyone stop you. He was really proud of his baby girl. As he got ready to leave, he said that he would be back later. Well, he was gone for about 5 minutes and my daughter received a text saying something had happened to him. Then his mom called saying we needed to come to the hospital. He had been shot. Before I could leave the house, she called and said that he had passed away.

I also received a call saying one of my twin daughters was in labor at the hospital around the same time. I had one daughter who had just had a baby, another one in labor, and the baby daddy was murdered...all in one day. I broke down. I didn't know what to do. I needed someone to come stay at the house with my daughter so that I could go check on my other daughter who was in the hospital, and also try to go be with the mom of my granddaughter dad. When I got to

I was being pulled in so many directions. She needed me, the one at home needed me, then his family needed me. I felt like Job; I had lost everything! When I returned home, my best friend had come over to console me. I was broken into pieces. All of this came at me all at once! She had to pray for me and help me try to keep it together. My daughter was having a mental breakdown. She had lost her grandmother a couple of months earlier.

I had recently gotten engaged. What was supposed to be a happy time for me really wasn't so happy. I was stricken with grief and had to make some hard decisions. I felt like everything was in turmoil. My daughter didn't want to look at or tend to the baby because she looked just like her dad; so I had to step in and help out. I had a business that I was running at the same time.

Granddaughter

-17-

DECISIONS AND SACRIFICES

-17-

Decisions and Sacrifices

I made the decision to take my business home. I am glad it was zoned for that, so I was able to obtain a business license. Now I could stay home to see about my daughter and granddaughter. I had an extra room in my house that I turned into a nail salon. It turned out good. I had a study clientele, and the shop looked really nice. I wasn't sure if my clients would want

I know with God all things are possible. Those things may not feel good, but it's working for my good. My boyfriend at the time had just proposed to me. The wedding plans were put on hold until I got my daughter stable. I kept her in church and the saints were praying for her. Within no time, she was getting better and she started doing things for her daughter. I would fix my granddaughter up and take her to church. She looked just like a precious doll. I can say that being at home wasn't bad at all. I started to see more money because I didn't have the business AND my home to take care of. I got more stuff done and my schedule was more flexible.

Pictures of my shop

-18-

THE WEDDING PLANS

-18-

The Wedding Plans

Things were getting back to normal, so I had time to plan my wedding. I had already chosen the wedding party as well as my colors. During the course of our relationship, I had seen some red flags, but I thought they would change once we got married. I was not in love with him at the time, and of course he knew. I thought I could grow to love him. I and some members were questioning me, asking me why I keep changing the date. They say he seems like a good guy. I told them I have finally set a date, which was May 20, 2012. I set the date 3 times and cancelled them due to issues I saw in him. The day came for us to get married. I had a lot of things running through my mind like, why am I doing this. I wasn't happy at all, but I didn't want to be embarrassed by not going through with it. When I was walking down the aisle to marry this man, one of the ladies looked at me and told me to smile. I knew I was making a mistake.

My best friend had planned a reception for us right after the wedding. It was decorated really nice. We had a nice time with all of our family and friends there. When it was over, we headed out to our honeymoon to Savannah, GA. We had a great time at the place I chose for us to go. The ride home wasn't pleasant at all. We had a disagreement about something. His attitude was horrible. When we got home, I threw my ring out the door and was annulled. I had spoken to the lady in the church who I called my mother. She had me to come to her house. We talked and she prayed with me and gave me some advice. When I returned home, he apologized and said he was going to fix it. So I gave him another chance.

We went for counsel with the pastor and things seemed to be getting better. My husband attended every church service and paid his tithes faithfully, but was a wolf in sheep's clothing. The church member thought he was a saint. The pastor made him a Deacon, and oh boy! I didn't always attend every church service. I had been a member there for 8 years and I was very faithful. He had only been going for over a year, and he came there only because I invited him to my church. He liked it and would come from time to time. He was a member of another church.

Wedding Picture

-19-

THE LAST STRAW

-19-

The Last Straw

He began to be verbally abusive, saying mean things just to hurt me. I discussed some of my past stuff that I was dealing with, and he would take that an use it against me. He opened up old wounds. When he did that, it made me very vulnerable and it hurt so bad. I thought when you say you love a person, you don't intentionally hurt months, then it was time to go. His attitude had gotten worse. The low down ways set in. I made a decision to leave town and go to Ohio to see my dad. He was having some medical problems and needed me.

When I started thinking about how things were playing out, I felt like he was jealous and was trying to destroy me and take everything I had away from me. I wasn't going to stay in Ohio. I was just going to get my dad situated. My husband had told me that if I left to not come back. When he got home, I told him I was going to Ohio, and he got so angry. I told him that I think it would be best if he left and stayed in his house until I left for Ohio, but he didn't want to; so I started packing his things.

He began to get physical by pushing and shoving me. He threw me over the chair, hurting my arm. He hit me in my face, bruising it. I called our Bishop and he told him to just leave. I was going to call the cops on him, because he started saying hurtful things to my daughter to me, I wanted so bad to call the cops and make him lose everything. But me being the person that I am, my heart is not built like that and I do have a conscience. I just let God deal with him. He can repay him far worse that I ever could (the Lord says, vengeance is mine, I will repay). There was absolutely no reconciling once you put your hand on me! That is a wrap! I had seen and witnessed abuse to the point of death, and I refuse to allow a man to think it is ok to put his hand on me!

Me with blonde hair

-20-

I DIDN'T LOOK BACK

-20-

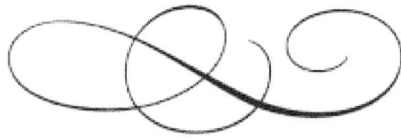

I Didn't Look Back

I left home December 22, 2012. I put my things in storage, and packed up my truck with what me and Nidica needed, and headed to Ohio. It took me about 16 hours to arrive. When we did, my daddy was so happy. I have always been his baby girl. Ohio was not what I expected. It snowed every day. I remember we got snowed in for several days. I wasn't used to that. I am a country girl! Nidica enjoyed the snow. She would go outside and play in it. My dad lived in the country. He had a lake with fish in it, some chicken, and a pig. It was like heaven to my baby girl. She loves animals. We saw real Amish people with the horse and buggy. I thought that was just on TV. We would go down to Warren, OH to visit with my 5 brothers by my daddy. We didn't have the same mother.

I was trying to drive in that snow. I was sliding off the road. I was one scared woman! I told daddy that since I had him situated with some things, when the weather broke, I was leaving. I didn't know where me and my baby girl were going, but I knew I was headed back down south. The north and snow wasn't for me.

We left at the end of February. We were going to stay in Tennessee or Atlanta; but since I was familiar with Atlanta, we stayed there. I didn't have a job when we got there. I had some money to last until I found one. We stayed in an Extended Stay hotel for a while. Our journey

Me and Nidica

You Can Make It!

You can't afford to give up or give in

You have people who love you

You have people depending on you

As long as you have breath in your body

Don't Give Up!!!

www.ingramcontent.com/pod-product-compliance
Lightning Source LLC
LaVergne TN
LVHW021515080426
835509LV00018B/2522